STAND

WOMAN

STAND!

(Second Edition)

*With Prayer, Patience, and Perseverance,
All things are Possible!*

*A Collection of True Inspirational Poetry
And Short Testimonials*

**By:
Valerie "Golden" Allen**

VJ Publishing House LLC.
3555 SW 90th Avenue
Miramar, FL 33025
www.vjpublishinghouse.com
Phone: 786-303-9551

Original Published: Author House 2/19/10
ISBN: 978-1-4490-8926-9 (sc)
       978-1-4490-8927-8 (e)
       978-1-4490-8925-2 (hc)

 Second Edition: VJ Publishing House LLC.
12/15/2015
ISBN: 978-1-939236-00-5

Library of Congress Control Number: 2010902121

Cover Design: Will Examara/Quick Prints
Fort Lauderdale, Florida
Printed in the United States of America

This book is printed on acid-free paper.

STAND

WOMAN

STAND!

(Second Edition)

"Special Dedication"
In Memory of My Friend:
Ms. Andrea Nugent

SOMETIMES...
Things happen to us that
we just don't understand

These things
SOMETIMES...
Become the door and
windows to our destiny

~Andrea Nugent~

"In Memory"

Although it was "So Deep" Judie,
and you've gone home to be with God,
I want to tell the World
you were the best mentor, friend,
and sister anyone could have been blessed with.
But most of all,
that Pillar of strength that taught me,
"I can do everything through Him
who gives me strength."
(Philippians 4:15 NIV)

I love you and yes, I'm still "STANDING!"

Table of Contents

"I know the plans I have for you," declares the Lord, *"plans to prosper you and not to harm you, plans to give you hope and a future."*
Jeremiah 29:11

~Introduction~

*Who am I? Well, I'm just like you, an individual who has probably gone through what you have, and then some. Now, I am going to make this introduction short, and to the point. Like myself, sometimes you don't even read the introduction, preface, or forward, you just jump right into the story. There are many books written on encouragement, inspiration, depression, obsession, tribulations, marriage, divorce, etc. But, I write for you who have suffered some, or even most of these challenges. I write about the **"Real Deal."** The spoken words through my poems and testimonials are true words of life, death, and resurrection. From broken to bankrupt, devastated to divorce, called forth to cancer, pain to promise, rejected to redemption, and victim to victor, I am evidence of God's wondrous works. He delivered me, saved me, freed me, healed me, but most of all; through it all, He kept me. Each poem and testimonial has an event or story behind it. Maybe a novel will tell more, but the Holy Spirit guided this process and I will obey. Hopefully if led, I will tell the whole story one day. But until then, read, receive, and believe this spiritually directed book. Remember, you must **STAND!** You are an **OVERCOMER!** And yes, you already have the **VICTORY!** I am truly evidence of that.*

Love, Valerie

Stand firm and you will see the deliverance
The Lord will bring you today.

Exodus 14:13

STAND WOMAN STAND!

STANDING
WAITING
TRUSTING
BELIEVING

CRYING
HOPING
PRAYING
RECEIVING

UNSURE OF YOUR PURPOSE
UNCLEAR ON WHAT TO DO
JUST PLAIN KNOWING
GOD HAS TAKEN CARE OF YOU

THE BATTLE'S BEEN TREACHEROUS
THE PAIN SOMETIMES DEEP
THOSE THICK DARK CLOUDS
HAS CAUSE YOU TO WEEP

WITH WEAPON IN HAND
YOU BEGIN TO SHOUT
BINDING UP EVIL
THAT TRIES TO COME ABOUT

STILL HOLDING ON
GASPING FOR AIR
TRUSTING IN THE END
HE'LL STILL BE THERE

WOMAN, KEEP ON STANDING
PERSEVERE, YES YOU CAN
YOU'RE GOD'S CHOSEN VESSEL
HIS PRECIOUS GIFT TO MAN

*"Therefore put on the full armor of God,
so that when the day of evil comes,
you may be able to stand your ground,
and after you have done everything, to Stand."
(Ephesians 6:13)*

[Part One]

The
Storm...

And when He got into the boat, His disciples
followed Him. And behold, there arose a great
storm in the sea, so that the boat was covered
with the waves; But He Himself was asleep. And
they came to Him saying, "save us Lord;
we are perishing!

Matthews 8:23-25

"When the Storm is Raging"

The stirring of the wind
Down pour of the rain
This storm that I'm in
Is a whirlwind of pain

Around and around
Feels like a tornado
Holding on for life
Not knowing if I'm able

Thunder and lightning
As treacherous as can be
These cares of life
Are getting the best of me

Oh, this is a bad one!
God please interfere
The way that it's looking
This may never clear

But after awhile
Things start to die down
The rain subsides
And settle on the ground

Gradually the sun
Peeks out its place of slumber
Replacing the dimness
And forecast I was under

Yes, Life storms
Will come and go
But God will deliver
For this I surely know

*And He got up and rebuked the wind and said to the sea
"Hush, be still". And the wind died down
and it became perfectly calm.
Mark 5:39*

Divine Set Up

I had ask for a change
To be given a new life
I felt I was ready
No matter what the price

But Satan had asked
For a test to prove my faith
To show that I would fail
And not finish the race

I was strong in words
My intentions of great
power
Face any warfare
Evilness I would devour

But oh! When it came
It hit me below the belt
It didn't play fair
I thought I'd lose myself

The suffering was so great
Don't know how I made it
through
I just believed
Nothing else could I do

Weeping and pleading
Knees bloody too
For it to be over
And my life renewed

Tattered and torn
Facing a breakdown
I can't explain that feeling
I just know I wasn't sound

I thought I was tough
No one could tell me so
Because I was a warrior
If only I had known

That evil nasty scoundrel
The master
of deceit
Would do all he did
To try and slay me

Let me tell you people
He's real, not a toy
He's on a mission
To kill, steal and destroy

But if you hold out
And pass the test
Your level of elevation
Will be worth the stress

So be careful what you say
And ask for too
Because the Father
of deceit
Is waiting to devour you

*"Your enemy the devil prowls around like a
roaring lion looking for someone to devour."
1 Peter 5:8-9*

Never Imagined

Looking back
Over the years
I never imagined
I would shed so many tears

Wrong choices
In and out's
Only God really knew
What it was about

As I mature
Through every situation
I am strengthen
Filled with motivation

To run on
Despite circumstance
Knowing it was He
Who gave me another chance

I never imagined
Didn't have a clue
About His Grace
And Mercy too

Now, I imagine
What waits for me
As I grasp hold of
My true destiny

"Let your light shine before men, that they may see your good deeds and praise your Faith in heaven." Matthew 5:16.

In His Arms

When life issues
Dominate you
And the billows
Are surging through
He will, care for you
Safe in His arms

When a barrage
Of storms and fears
And you have cried
A river of tears
He will, hide you
Safe in His arms

When you have tried
To press pass the pain
And all you feel
Is thunderous rain
He will, protect you
Safe in His arms

When you have felt
Like giving up
Thinking all you have
Is bad luck
He will, hold you
Safe in His arms

Please;
You must understand
For you
He has
A better plan
Don't throw in the towel
Take a stand!
He will keep you
Safe in His arms

"I will instruct you and teach you in the way you should go." Psalm: 32:8

"The Diagnosis"

"I'm so sorry"
Were the words the Doctor spoke
"You're going to be okay
You must have hope

You're a strong woman
With a whole lot more to give
Now it's up to you
If you want to die or live"

I was in shock
In total disbelief
Thinking, why would Jesus allow
This to happen to me

I never thought
In my wildest imagination
I would be faced
With this type of situation

So I decided
To throw a big party
Its theme would be "pity"
Attended by one body

The music was wailing
The dancing, un-balanced
Tears would be the beverage
Filled with lots of anguish

It wasn't fun
In fact it was sad
Should've never attended
It turned out really bad

The **Diagnosis** was 'Cancer'
A deadly disease
That sickens and kills
Bringing many to their knees

But if you have faith
And stand supreme
No matter what the diagnosis
Jesus is the King!

He is the Healer!
Of all the healers!
Standing for you
Just like a Pillar

So catch your breath
And go to your Friend
Jesus will support you
And help you win

Yes, you got to fight
Give it everything you got!
This battle is the Lord's
But you must do your part

*Then they cry unto the Lord in their trouble and He
saveth them out of their distresses.
Psalm 107:19*

"Bargain"

If you do this
Then I'll do that
As I tried to compromise
To wear a different hat

I'll do whatever you want me to do
Say whatever you want me to say
Please Heavenly Father
Just take it all away

This news is unbearable
The diagnosis a dream
All I remember
Is how loud I screamed

Saying," I'm too young
I still have work to do!"
I tried to negotiate
For my life to be new

That life I took for granted
The sins that I commit
The half-foot inside church
And all my little tricks

Had caught up with me
Ms. Know it all
But this situation
Has literally made me fall

I tried to bargain
With the Father up above
He just made one statement
"You're the one I love"

Deal or no deal
In Him I put my trust
It's going to be okay
I 'll just have to adjust

God said, "I will be with you." Exodus 3:12

"Spoken Words"

The words were so clear, that turbulent night
As I lie in my tears, with no strength to fight

Unable to sleep, too much on my mind
At my wits end, feeling life's been unkind

Worn out and weary, of the warfare and the pain
It seems like every day, all I feel is rain

But in a moment, in the twinkling of an eye
When He spoke those words, my tears began to dry

He said
"Where is your faith?
Why are you worried?"
As I cried out to Him, to come in a hurry

Jesus made a way, out of no way at all
He heard my plea!
He answered my call!

Oh! How I love Him, he is real and not a toy
My Beloved Savior, the one that I adore

For He has not despised or disdained the suffering of the
afflicted one; He has not hidden His face from him but has
listened to his cry for help.
Psalm 22:24

MERCY... said No!

Gasping for air
What's happening to me?
Is this it?
Will I be history?

Haven't finish the assignments
There is still too much to do
Was my work in vain?
Am I really through?

Heavenly Father
What's going on?
Is this my appointed hour?
Could I have been wrong?

If it's not your will
Please intervene
This doesn't feel right
Is this all a dream?

Satan has been after me
Because Its you that I serve
He's trying to take me out
He really has the nerve

Father it doesn't matter
My life hasn't been in vain
Suffering for your kingdom
Is part of the pain

But **MERCY**... stepped in
To death, it said No!
Blew life back into me
And opened up the door

I'm back on assignment
Shouting to and fro
Telling the world about Jesus
Everywhere I go

But, because of His Mercy. Titus 3:5

"In The Trenches"

Fighting for my life
My world is upside down
Don't know if I can survive
Another round

I'm in the trenches
Living undercover
Surrounded by enemies
Stuck in a gutter

This battle...
Is too much to endure
Cleanse me Father
Make my life pure

I got to trust You
No matter what
This thing call life
Seems a bit too much

So pull me out
Extend Your hand
This pit is too deep
For me to understand

I now realize
You were always near
When I surrendered
All things became clear

Never will I doubt
What You can do for me
Because of Your mercy
I'm now set free!

*O God the Lord, the strength of my salvation, thou hast
covered my head in the day of battle.
Psalm 140:7*

In My Window

How do you know?
You weren't there
I confided in no one
This I swear!

Trials and tribulations
Ups and downs
God's my only witness
No one else was around

Did you peep in my window?
Crack open the door?
It was top secret
This I can assure

Challenges of life
Heartaches and pain
Sometime out my window
All I see is rain

Trying not to lean
To things I don't comprehend
Trusting in His word
No more listening to man

Most times the good
Does out weigh the bad
It will get better
This I understand

So when you look in my window
Be sure of what you see
Because you really don't know
What's going on inside me

God blesses the people who patiently endure testing.
Afterward they will receive the crow of life that God has
promised to those who love Him.
James 1:12

Going Through, Again!

Here we go!
He's at it again
That evil scoundrel
Simply isn't my friend

Up at his hour
Plotting his next attack
Trying to find a way
To throw me off track

Up and down
Like a rollercoaster ride
It's difficult to perceive
That I'm still alive

Sometimes it's so hard
I don't know what to do
I feel confused
Like that lady in the shoe

I will find a way
To persevere
Because I wasn't born
With the spirit of fear

So, as I go through
I know God's by my side
Ordering my steps
Being my guide

I will serve Him
Until my last breath
He is my Father
He is my Help

How that in a great trial of affliction the abundance of their joy and their deep poverty abounded into the riches of their liberality.
2 Corinthians 8:2

Rescue Me!

Like rolling waves
Toss side to side
I'm in need of a navigator
To be my guide

This here water...
Is too deep
Throw me a lifeline
I can't compete

The rough tides
And unsettled wind
I call for an anchor
To pull me in

For I am weary
Tired of the hold
Father I surrender
Body, spirit, and soul

I have tried
To do it my way
But I keep messing up
Day after day

Slowly sinking
Please don't let me drown
Rescue me Lord!
I know you're still around

I need Your power
You are my only hope
Save me Lord!
Help me stay afloat

*And though the waves thereof toss themselves, yet can they
not prevail; though they roar, yet they cannot pass over it.
Jeremiah 5:22*

Suicide

What could have been so awful
that caused you to not want to breathe anymore?

What was it that made you
give up on you?

What happened, to make you feel
you didn't owe yourself, others or God
another chance?

What in heaven's name, pushed you
into isolation, confinement, seclusion
were you thought, there was no way out?

What over powered your mind, body, and soul
and made you not want to search for a glimpse of light,
in the midst of all that darkness?

What robbed you of life
its essence, its worth, its significance,
it's meaning of love, liberty, and freedom without charge?

Please...
Tell me why?
Tell me what?
Tell me how?
Did you decide
"You"
Didn't deserve to exist anymore...

You left me
You left you
You left life
I guess I'll never know
Why?

*To give light to them that sit in darkness and in the
shadow of death, to guide our feet
into the way of peace.
Luke 1:79*

The *Ride*

Riding the route
To the final resting place
All I could think of
Was when I last saw your face

Those memories
Flooding my mind
Are scattered pictures
Playing in rewind

I now know that it's real
And not just a facade
Because of what I'm feeling
Deep in my heart

No longer can I imagine
Or feel your touch
This death thing
Seems a little too much

The *Ride*
Quite and slow
Makes me question
The things that I know

Emotions and thoughts
Overtakes my mind
Erasing spoken words
"That everything will be fine"

This void
So empty and hallow
Is the biggest pill
I ever had to swallow

The *Ride*
Is coming to an end
As I finally realize
This is real, not pretend

Take your rest...

I will dwell in the House of the Lord, forever. Psalm 23

"Rain"

The rain keeps falling
When will it stop?
With tissue in hand
I absorb every drop

What is wrong with me?
Why can't I forget?
My best interest
He never meant

Forever mine...
I thought He would be
Loving him so hard
I lost a part of me

I have got to find a way
To finally let go
Stop all this grieving
God has more for me in store

The sun will shine again
This rain will eventually stop
Everything is going to work out
I feel it in my heart

When the Lord saw her, His heart went out to her
and He said, "Don't cry."
Luke 7:1

Express your deepest thoughts:

1. Which poem was your favorite? Why?

2. Which poem can you relate to? How?

3. What poem inspired you the most?

Notes:

[Part Two]

Blinded by The Storm...

We are hard pressed on every side, but not crushed: perplexed, but not in despair; persecuted, but not abandoned; struck down, but not destroyed.

2nd Corinthians 4:8

"Let It Go"

I've tried so hard
But I continuously fail
This sin that I'm in
Can send me to hell

Why does it feel right?
When I know that it's wrong
It's against His laws
How long can it go on?

God's been so good
Allowing me to sort things out
He's given me every chance
To take a different route

My heart says yes
My mind tells me no
I'm trying to do what's right
But the flesh won't let go

This is so painful
I don't know what to do
My soul is crying out
Father, I'm confused

I must let go
I have to sacrifice
For all of my sins
You've paid the price

I will let go
I shall do what's right
My eyes are open now
I finally see the light

God is faithful; He will not let you be tempted beyond what you can bear. But when you are tempted, He will also provide a way out.
1 Corinthians 10:13

You Too?

Somehow, I'm not surprised
You came my way
Been-there, done-that
The game continues to be played

It's so funny
You knew all the moves
Did just about everything
To try and make me lose

No matter what
I won't change my mind
I'll always serve Him
Until the end of time

There goes another one!
That Satan would use
To try and abort my destiny
To make me stand accused

Of being a failure
Who couldn't pass the test
Nor rise above pain
Or triumph over stress

Huh! You really are crazy
I know who died for me
So until my last breath
I will serve all three

Father, Son, and Holy Spirit
Even help mankind too
This is part of my purpose
Righteousness I choose

Please understand
It was never about you
It's all about Him
For God anything, I'll do

Forgive us for our sins. Luke 11:4

"Double-Life"

Lies
Deceit
Deception
Defeat

A wife and a lover
Living in duress
You've cause so much suffering
Leaving behind a mess

A halo you bore
Clothed in disguise
Said that you love me
And for me, you'd even die

Tell me why?
I was innocent
What could I have done?
This doesn't make sense

Another blow
Heartbreak knows my name
God please tell me why
I have to endure so much pain?

To you...
It was all a game
Living life on the double
Has bought nothing but shame

I Am Done...

But He answered and said unto them, An evil and
adulterous generation seeketh after a sign;
and there shall no sign be given to it.
Matthew 12:39

Betrayed

I open my life to you…

I allowed you to
Climb over the wall
Without a ladder

You knew better than anyone
What I have been through

Humiliated and shame
I now reside in a residence call
"Hurt"

I said I would never live there
Again...

I tried to protect myself
But here I am
Dealing with landlord abuse

I will vacate this **condemned** property
And never look back

Betrayed, yes
Heart broken, yes
But someday
A loving new home
Will become vacant
And with open arms
It will welcome me in

Home Sweet Home…

They delight in lies: they bless with their mouth, but they
curse inwardly. Selah...
Psalm 62:4

"In Sheep Clothing"

In collar and robe you came
Sweeping me off my feet
Caught me at a time
I was vulnerable and weak

A wolf in sheep clothing
On assignment in disguise
A so call man of God
Filled with lots of pride

A scholar of the word
From Genesis to Revelation
Claim your love for Jesus
In our conversations

Cunning and crafty
A pretender undercover
It's amazing how you believe
You'll never be discovered

It's really sad
How you are so blind and lost
Deeply in denial
Not caring what it cost

I don't feel remorseful
For what's headed your way
Because you are aware
Of what the word says

Please get it right
Fast, pray, and repent
Stop playing church
Or to hell, you'll be sent!

If an enemy were insulting me, I could endure it; if a foe were raising himself against me, I could hide from him. But it is you, a man like myself, my companion, and my close friend.
Psalm 55:12-13

"TIN-MAN"

I thought he only exist
In the Wizard of Oz
All that tin man wanted
Was to be given
a heart

You know,
It's that muscle
That carries blood
Throughout your body
And offers out love

What is that echo
I hear in your chest?
A sound so hallow
That has put me
In distress

Who created you?
Mister Man of steel
A being unable to love
An entity unable to feel

You are a rare one
So vicious and cold
Filled with hate
and anger
Did you sell your soul?

I tried hard to love you
And help you
understand
It doesn't take all that
Just be a real man

But no, you're
a coward
Who have hurt
so many
An evil
Malicious person
Who doesn't
have heart for any

It's hard for you
to accept
What I have to say
But it is the truth
Mister
you need to pray

This isn't easy for you
But please come to
God
He is the only Deliverer
That can give you
A new heart

I the Lord search the heart and examine
the mind, to reward a man according to
his conduct, according to what his
deeds deserve." Jeremiah 17:10

Stand Down!

Lurking in the darkness
Searching for souls
You Evil Scoundrel!
You are exposed!

Enemy of the light
Prowling around
In the name of the Father
It's time you "stand down!"

To kill, steal, and destroy
It's your ultimate goal
You've been defeated
Now let Gods people go

"Stand Down!"
You think you are so tough
Your days are numbered
Enough is enough!

Now you and your clan
Return to your mess
Because you have been conquered
By righteousness

*Put on the full armor of God so that you can take your stand
against the devil's schemes.
Ephesians 6:11*

"PERPETRATOR"

Covered in Disguise
Who could this be?
This perpetrator
That stands before me

Tell me who you are!
Person of deceit
What in heaven's name
Are you trying to do to me?

I only wanted to help
Prayed your deliverance too
You said "stop trying to save me
I'll do whatever I want to do"

You're such a phony
Oh you hypocrite!
Don't you remember the promise?
How could you forget?

His call, you said you'll answer
Myself, I said it too
But when the storms came
You couldn't follow through

You forgot what He's done
And how He blessed you so
Gave you another chance
I for one should know

I pray one day you get it
Believing He's all that you need
Because the one that you're serving
Is a Liar, yes indeed

God is faithful; He will not let you be tempted beyond what
you can bear. 1 Corinthians 10:13

Below The Belt

We are not getting along
Divorce is on the way
Why would you use our children?
To try and make me pay

I never thought
You would stoop so low
You really know how
To throw a nasty blow

These are our kids
Not some game
As a matter-of-fact
You should be ashamed!

All the terrible things
You've said and done
Don't you even have respect?
For our daughter and son

You need to take a look
At yourself
Stop acting like a fool
And get some help

So watch what you say
And what you do
That ditch you dug for me
Could very well be for you

God is against the proud, but he gives grace
to the humble.
1 Peter 5:5

Divorcee

Why did it
Come to this?
We were a family
For a while in bliss

I never thought
We would ever separate
The papers are signed
It's now too late

Shattered dreams
So much pain
I now realize
Loving you was in vain

You said I was forever
My heart you would carry
So deeply in love
You wanted to marry

What really happen
To make you change your mind?
Here I'm thinking
It would all work out fine

Yes;
We are now divorce
I hope you're able
To live with your choice

But it's all good
True love awaits me
I will survive
Just you wait and see

They won't be afraid of bad news;
their hearts are steady because they trust the Lord.
Psalm 112:7

Down Low

I had no idea
I was living a lie
You were undercover
Hidden in disguise

On the down low
Living a secret life
Fooled by a fool
Thought I would be your wife

Double-crossed
Misled and betrayed
It's still hard to believe
I was totally played

Sucker punched
Knock the breath out of me!
I never thought
I would pay such a fee

What was done in the dark
Has surface to the light
I sometimes wonder
Do you sleep at night?

But, it's all good
It's your loss
I'm a strong woman
Jesus is my boss!

So long Perpetrator!
I now can honestly say
I wish you well
In the most genuine way

Anyone who claims to live in God's light and hates
a brother or sister is still in the dark.
1 John 2

COVER

I knew it was
something
Couldn't put my
finger on it
The one that I loved
Was in concealment

So charismatic
and friendly
He caught me
off guard
You see I was in the
process
Of healing from
a broken heart

So I went out
on a limb
Thinking I finally
found forever
When it all went down
I had married the
DEVIL!

My mind was
confused
Filled with so many
thoughts
I didn't want
to believe
So against it I fought

A woman like me
Could never be so
blind
I'm too intelligent
Labeled fine as wine

It would take
a few years
For the truth to
come out
A lying
Evil imposter
Had me living
a life of doubt

Our relationship
Was totally a hoax
He was undercover
Known as
"The Down Low"

It's truly amazing
How darkness comes
to light
It wasn't my fault
I tried to do right

I now understand
How it feels
To be dealt
A really bad deal...

*"I will restore health unto you and I will
heal all your wounds."
Jeremiah 30:17*

35

I Let Her Get Away

If I can turn back
The hands of time
Things will be different
She will be mine

A heartless fool
Egotistic and cavalier
I was a simpleton
Who didn't respect her tears

So arrogant
It was all about me
I was on top of the world
Blind and could not see

That power and pride
Money and fame
If not handled right
Could lead to shame

Disheartened
Lonely and sad
Why didn't I realize
What I had?

If I had one more chance
To do it over again
I will be different
And make amends

But, I have lost her
She's moved on
I'm suffering the consequences
Now that she's gone

If the way you live isn't consistent with what you believe,
then it's wrong.
Romans 14:2

I Wonder...

I wonder what it's like
To bask in the bliss
To feel complete
And my love not remiss

I wonder what it's like
To anticipate the sensation
That when we are together
It's always a celebration

I wonder what it's like
To be the apple of someone's eye
Will I ever know that feeling?
Before I die?

I wonder what it's like
To experience reciprocity
Knowing the love is mutual
No question of security

I wonder what it's like
To encounter ageless love
Ensured by his embrace
This was sent from above

I really do wonder
If any of this is ideal
Or am I blinded by cliché
And real love is surreal

I do wonder...

A merry heart maketh a cheerful countenance.
Proverbs 15:13

"Open My Heart"

Can I trust you?
If I give you my heart
Handle it with care
From the very start

Will you preserve it?
Like fruit in a jar
Can you light it up?
Like the morning star

For it has been broken
Crushed and frayed too
Tossed from side to side
Changed from red to blue

It desires true love
And cries out for joy
To be treated tenderly
Not played like a toy

Can I really trust you?
If I let you in
Will you be real?
And not pretend

Should I take a chance?
On you treating me right
Fulfilling my everything
Morning, noon and night

Don't know if I can trust you
Or be able to exhale
I really do want to
But time will only tell

The grass withers and the flowers fall, but the
word of the Lord stands forever.
1 Peter 1:24-25

Karma

They say it's known
To come around again
It's called "payback"
At the expense of sins

Karma
Expression or consequence
To me none of it
Make any sense

In actuality
Does the sole doer fall?
Is it indicative?
Of what it's called

Is it an effect?
Of the cause
Punishment or chastisement
For it all

To judge;
Is not my plight
Nor to decide
What's wrong or right

We are all born with
Free will and choice,
To act liberally
And express through voice

Karma

A repayment
Of the things you have did

Jesus called Judas friend
when he was about to betray Him. Matthew 26

Express your deepest thoughts:

1.Which poem was your favorite?
Why?

2. Which poem can you relate to?
How?

3. What poem inspired you the most?

Notes:

[Part Three]

Riding Through The Storm...

And we know that all things work together for good to them that love God, to them who are called according to His purpose.

Romans: 8:28

"So Deep"

How far down
Do I have to go?
Before I'm delivered
From all the blows

One after the other
All *"So Deep"*
Filled with so much pain
Until I can barely speak

It's surreal
Like I'm in a dream
This feeling inside
Makes me want to scream

About all my trials
And tribulations too
You wouldn't understand
Unless it happened to you

I've cried a river
I've prayed and fast
I've given so much
I'm down to my last

But, I must hold on
To His unchanging hand
Believing for me
He has the perfect plan

So, no more complaining
Grace will see me through
I have to keep on standing
Nothing else can I do

***Pray continually; give thanks in all circumstances,
for this is God's will for you in Christ Jesus.
1 Thessalonians 5:17-18***

"I Must Tell"

Yes, you were that button
The enemy chose to press
Releasing such an explosion
Leaving everything a mess

Now I must tell
How Jesus rescued me
Oh no, I'll never hold
This testimony

From Africa to Asia
Middle East and Russia too
This word I have inside
I will shout until I am through

Around the world I'll go
For Jesus, I will do
Never unpacking my suitcase
Until He tells me to

God is absolutely amazing
Like me, you He will save
All you do is trust Him
And give Him all the praise!

Listen…this is for real
In Him there are no games
If you turn it over to Jesus
You'd never be the same

Grasp hold of what I'm saying
From God don't refrain
Because the Devil is a liar!
It's simply, that plain

I will praise You, O Lord, with all my heart; I will tell
of all your wonders.
Psalm 9:1

"The Cord"

Holding on
Suspended in air
Twisting and twirling
Life hasn't been fair

Rocking and reeling
As dizzy as can be
Feeling like a leaf
Swaying on a tree

I won't let go
I'll never release
This cord of life
That has sustained me

My hands are bloody
Blistered and bruised
From holding too tight
I'm paying my dues

This cord of life
Now withered and worn
Has held me up
Since I was born

Satan continues
To try and cut me down
But I am determined
I'm getting my crown!

I'll keep holding on
Until He pulls me in
Then I'll walk around heaven
With Jesus, my Friend

*Do not fear, I am with you; do not be dismayed, for I
am your God... I will strengthen you and help you;
I will uphold you with My righteous right hand."
Isaiah 41:10*

Midlife Crisis

I gave myself to you
For so many years
Now you want to walk away
Leaving me in tears

What about the vows?
The children and our home
I thought we were forever
Evidently, I was wrong

"You need to find yourself"
Were the words you spoke
Leaving me pleading, begging
Holding on to hope

That you would come back
To realization
Take a stand, be a man
And fix this situation

I don't know what to do
Or else can I say
To get you to understand
It's only just a phase

It's call mid-life crisis
A place of confusion and doubt
That leaves you with this feeling
That you are missing out

Although this is very hard
For me to take or accept
I will continue to pray
That you find yourself

And I said, Oh that I had wings like a dove!
For then would I fly away, and be at rest.
Psalm 55:6

Reflection

Who is that?
Staring at me
Where did she come from?
Who could she be?

The woman in the mirror
A face I can't define
Filled with obscurity
Imperfect by time

Challenges of life
Have all set in
That woman in the mirror
Can no longer pretend

Face-to-face
She must realize
Her key to happiness
Lies deep inside

With a desire
To be set free
The woman in the mirror
Could she be me?

Woman in the mirror
It's just a matter of time
With God all things are possible
You will be fine

A devout life does bring wealth,
but it's the rich simplicity of being yourself
before God.
1 Timothy 6:6

"Façade"

Why can't I enjoy this?
I have waited so long
Thinking, *finally happiness*
But again, only heartbreak

My cries are mourns
Turned into muffled whimpers
Filled with anguish
Distorted by tomorrow

Pretending
To be me
When the mirror is reflective
Of what is real

Should I face her?
Could I face her?
Can I change her?
God, help her!

She is me...

And rejoice in the hope of the Glory of God. Not only so, but we also rejoice in our sufferings, because we know that suffering produces perseverance; perseverance, character; and character, hope."
Romans 5:2-

"What About Me?"

Through all this hardship
And adversity
The trials of life
Has taken its toll on me

In the midst of it all
As I gasp for breath
Sometimes thinking
"This is worse than death"

Praying and Fasting
Can I have some relief?
Father in Heaven
Have you abandoned me?

It's so difficult
To see your face
I'm really going through
Will I finish this race?

Rock me in your bosom
Hold me like a babe
I need you Father
To deliver and to save

Is it only me
Wounded in this way?
Please intervene
Don't let me go astray

You're the only source
That I can run to
Rescue me Lord
And make my life brand new

God said, "I will be with you."
Exodus 3:12

"In Myself"

The way that I feel
Words can't express
This broken spirit
This soul in distress

The women in me
Cries out for relief
Desiring to be heard
And granted some peace

Trial after trial
One after the other
She's got to find a way
To recover

The lady inside
Who's in so much pain
Can't figure out
Why there's so much rain

When will it stop
It's coming down hard
I'm so weary and tired
Please help me Lord!

The little girl within
That still plays hide-n-seek
Yearns to be held
Behind every defeat

Woman, lady, girl
We are we
Balancing each other
Until eternity

"When you pass through the waters, I will be with you; and when you pass through the rivers, they will not sweep you. When you walk through the fire, you will not be burned...for I am the Lord, Your God."
Isaiah 43:2-3

He Kept Me

Struggle after struggle
Defeat on top of defeat
Trials and tribulations
They've all made me weak

But, I have a refuge
One that I can claim
I'm standing on His word
And it has kept me sane

Through every situation
And circumstance of life
I remember the blood
I can't forget the price

Though sometimes it gets hard
I wonder, "What should I do?"
Again I hear a whisper
Saying, "I will never forsake you"

I'm His chosen daughter
The one that He saved
Because of His touch
I'm strong, bold and brave

Yes, Jesus **kept me**
Time and time again
I'll continue to trust Him
With that, I'm sure to win

*You will keep in perfect peace him whose mind is
steadfast, because He trust in You.
Isaiah 26:*

This Too Shall Pass...

Looking through my purse
Searching all the drawers
Checking pants pockets
Hoping to find a few dollars

Its dinnertime
There is no rice or meat
This is getting hard
We can barely eat

No money in the bank
Nor a cent on credit too
Lord I need a blessing
Tell me what to do?

The enemy is at work
Trying to break me down
But I'm holding on
I know you're still around

You have never forsaken me
I know this is just a test
I will continue to stand
And give you my best

This too shall pass...
I will make it through
Then I will be elevated
And receive the promises too

"I am the bread of life. He who comes to Me will
never go hungry, and he who believes in Me,
will never be thirsty."
John 6:35

Express your deepest thoughts:

1. **Which poem was your favorite? Why?**

2. **Which poem can you relate to? How?**

3. **What poem inspired you the most?**

Notes:

[Part Four]

What I Told The

Storm...

The Lord is my light and salvation; whom shall I fear? The Lord is the strength of my life; of whom shall I be afraid?

Psalm 27:1

Violated

You were so kind
Treated me nice
Not for a moment
Did I think
twice

That my purity
Would be betrayed
Touched...
In the most indecent
way

Untainted
Virtuous and free
Suddenly disturbed
By, my family

A predator
In disguise
Robbed me
Of my precious side

Lavished...
With goods and treats
In my heart
I thought you were
sweet

A stripping
Of innocence
Snatched away
Under the wrong
pretense

Filled with fear
And uncertainty
If I told on you
Would anyone
believe?

A prisoner
Of myself
I now believe its time
I get some help

Set free!
From guilt and shame
I never deserve
All that pain

No more!
Will I take the blame
You *Violated* me!
You left your stain!

So from this day forth
I erase what you did
I'm now all Woman
Not that scared little
kid...

*For God will bring every deed into
judgment, including every hidden thing.
Ecclesiastes 12:14*

"Woman In Distress"

Oh no you didn't!
Have you lost your mind?
You've went too far
Just crossed the line

Put your hands on me
Touch me the way you did
Oh now it's really on
Listen, I'm not your kid!

Oh, you're a brave one
Do you know who I am?
I wasn't raised this way
And really don't give a damn!

I won't call 911
No need to compromise
I will just call my people
To get you out my life!

So, go on about your business
While I'm still in control
I'm trying not to lose it
You really are a bold soul

Listen Boy!
I know where you come from
Get out of my face
Matter of fact, you better run!

This is finished!
You went too far!
Just leave me alone
And give me back my heart

When I called, you answered me; you made me bold and
stouthearted.
Psalm 138:3

I Won't Quit

It's been so hard
Don't know what to do!
No one
Could've walked in these shoes

Blistered and bruised
Trying to find my way
Pressing on
Struggling not to stray

Should I go east?
When the sign points west
I'm in need of a guide
To lead me where's best

Girded up in armor
I am suited for every round
I've got to make it!
I will get my crown!

Oh yes,
I deserve it
It's been promised
I will not quit

No matter what
I shall remain
Forever in His arms
Despite all the pain...

Without wavering, let us hold tightly to the hope we say we have, for God can be trusted to keep His promise.
Hebrews 10:23

Fight On!

It's in me
The will to fight
Enough of this mess
I know my rights

To be happy
Forever free
Thrive in my doing
To just be me

With every knock down
I will rise again
Back in the ring
Determine to win

Bruised and battered
A wound here or there
I won't give up
This I swear

Oh Yes!
It's a duel of a match
I'm not throwing in the towel
God's got my back

So bring it on!
I'm covered in the blood
I am Champion!
His instrument of love

Finally, be strengthen by the Lord and by His vast strength.
Ephesians 6:10

Don't Take It!

You say that I should forgive you
Turn the other cheek, and trust you again
Forget the verbal abuse, rage, and strike too
Keep my lips sealed, and stay

Consumed with fear
Concerned for my life
I consider what I hear
For the sake of our love, our family

I never imagined, my love at my throat
Or that my face, would be bruised
Still I love you, with hope
Confused about what really is enough

Do I stay, or do I go?
For better, or for worst
Till death do us part
Must I sacrifice, my well being for you?

Like a prisoner, I feel trapped
Afraid I may not survive, your next attack
In the midst of your fury, I notice a stranger
No love, no soul, no compassion in your eyes

The value of my life, is too high
This can't be love; I must find a way out
On my knees I pray
"Yea though I walk through the valley of the shadow of death"

God has not given me the spirit of fear
I must break free!
I will break free!
This cannot be my destiny!

I won't cover up my bruises
I won't make excuses
I will tell the truth, and stand strong
I won't take it!

"Do not fear, for I am with you." Isaiah 41:30

Dead Weight

Why you holding on?
To all that dead weight
It's time to let it go
Before it's too late

Aren't you tired?
Of carrying that load?
Barely holding yourself up
If the truth be told

That extra baggage
Is weighing you down
If you keep lugging it
You may not be around

It doesn't belong to you
Now, give it back!
Return to **SENDER**
As a matter-of-fact

You got your own issues
To deal with
Enough is enough
It's time to quit

Now, move on
You deserve a break
Simply just get rid of
All that dead weight

Get rid of all bitterness, rage, anger, harsh words, and
slander, as well as all types of malicious behavior.
Ephesians 4

No More!

No more over counter aids
No swallowing of pills
No glasses of wine
To take away what I feel

No more sleepless nights
No cries in the dark
No wondering why
I allow you to break my heart

No more turning the cheek
No trying to understand
No pleading and begging
For you to be a real man

No more of your lies
No being discreet
No carrying your baggage
Nor your secrets will I keep

I've put up with your stuff
For the very last time
Enough is enough!
Now it's time to get mine

You didn't deserve me
Should've never let you in
Now that it's over
No more will I pretend

The way of a fool seems right to him,
but a wise man listens to advice.
Proverbs 12:15

"Enough Said"

Everyone is trying
To run my life
Giving their opinion
That I take their advice

Saying "things will get better
Just you wait and see
God has a plan for you
Like He had for me"

I try hard to listen
To what they have to say
But they don't understand
All I want to do is pray

Over and over
I cry for help
For Him to do His will
Cause I don't trust myself

I appreciate their words
And compassion too
But He's the only solution
To what I'm going through

No matter what is happening
I've got to persevere
Cause in my darkest hour
It's His voice I need to hear

Your statues are my delight; they are my Counselors.
Psalm 119:24

"It Doesn't Matter"

Criticized, mistreated
Scrutinized and scorned
Lied, cheated on
Tattered and torn

They're talking about me
Everywhere I turn
But it doesn't matter
God's who I yearn

Saying things that hurt
And belittle me so
They've never walked in my shoes
Or felt those nasty blows

Deliverance hasn't been easy
Yes, it took awhile
For me to believe
I was His chosen child

He is my Father
The one that I trust
They can never comprehend
What we have between us

I've matured now
Words don't hurt anymore
On Him I depend
Because He is the door

So go on, keep talking
As He lifts me up
He is my Savior
That fills my cup

"Blessed are you when people insult you,
persecute you and falsely say all kinds of evil against you
because of Me."
Matthews 5:11

"THE CALL"

Here we go again
Aren't you a little tired?
Haven't you gotten it?
Do you have any pride?

Find something else to do
Go on get a life!
I owe everything to Him
For me, He's paid the price

You've tampered with my finances
Bought shame to my name
Stole my husband
Making me the blame

Sent sickness to my family
Cause me a scare or two
Tried to take my mind
But Jesus wouldn't let you

My blessed Savior
He is the only way
In Him I will put my trust
And continue to pray

Sometimes I may stumble
And even fall
But I am still that woman
Whose answered "**THE CALL**"

The Lord is near to all who call on Him,
to all who call on Him in truth.
Psalm 145:18

Haters

They call you goodie-two shoes
Envying your life
Those so call haters
Don't understand the price

Not knowing what you've been through
Don't care to hear your story
Desiring your possessions
Trying to steal your glory

Exposed evildoers
Conspire to see you fall
Plotting, lying, scheming
Wishing your back against the wall

But don't you dare worry
Go ahead let them hate
You see no one can stop
What God elevates

Remember, it's necessary
For them to stir up mess
Be forever grateful
Because of them you're bless

With head held high
Continue that climb
Strive for greatness
You're one of a kind

Anyone who claims to live in God's light and hates
a brother or sister is still in the dark.
1 John 2:9

"Give It To God"

What's this sensation?
Deep within my heart
I'm so tired of hurting
Will it ever stop?

I've tried and tried
To live and do right
But seem like everyday
I face a brand new fight

Heavenly Father
For a minute stop by
I'm so weary and worn
Don't you hear my cries?

You said in your word
All I had to do was call
Father I'm pleading
I'm about to fall!

Only you know
How much I can bear
This load is so heavy
Please help me share

Suffer for your kingdom
That, I will do
But I need a little help
And guidance too

The way that I'm feeling
Words can't express
I do wonder
Will I ever pass the test?

I'm going to make it!
Somehow I will
All of these burdens
To you, I willingly give

"Come to Me, you who are weary and burdened." Matt 11:28

This Won't Break Me!

I will stand tall as a tower
Strong as rolling seas
This situation
Will not break me!

Everything…
Seems out of control
I won't give in
I am Bold!

All those fiery darts
That's been cast my way
Will not penetrate
Do you hear what I say?

Yes, it formed
But it won't prosper
I'm the head not the tail
Now that is gospel!

You thought you had me
Caught up in a snare
Please understand
I believe in the power of prayer

This won't break me!
I will persevere
My God has not given me
The spirit of fear

God blesses the people who patiently endure testing.
Afterward, they will receive the crown of life that God has
promised to those who love Him.
James 1:12

Ninety-Nine

Ninety-nine's, not enough
Oh no, It won't do
God want it all
That includes you

Every single thing
You must freely give
The good and the bad
No matter how it feel

Even when you wonder
And question, why?
Just accept His answer
And give it a try

Run that race
Finish the course
Sometimes falling
But get back up!

Remember every step
He's by your side
Covering and protecting
When the pains too much to hide

One hundred percent
Ninety-nine, just won't do
He wants everything
And that includes you

*Love the Lord your God, Listen to His voice,
and hold fast to Him.
Deuteronomy 30:20*

Say, Yes!

Can you stand the pain?
When you're being pressed
Trusting in Him
And still say yes

Yes, to His will
Yes, to His way
Yes, to His word
Yes, everyday

Yes, through the good
Yes, when things are bad
Yes, when you're happy
Yes, even when you're sad

Yes, in the sunshine
Yes, when it rain
Yes, when you're joyful
Yes, through the pain

Yes, when you're strong
Yes, when you're weak
Yes, when there's silence
Yes, when you speak

Yes, when its points right
Yes, when told to go left
Yes, to life
Yes, to death

I'll always say yes
How can I say no?
He is my everything
Yes, He is the door

Choose for yourselves this day whom you will serve.
Joshua 24:15

Express your deepest thoughts:

1. Which poem was your favorite? Why?

2. Which poem can you relate to? How?

3. What poem inspired you the most?

Notes:

[Part Five]

*Over Coming
The Storm...*

*Because he hath set his love upon me, therefore
will deliver him; I will set him on high, because he
hath known my name.*

Psalm 91:14

Get Out

Trapped, you thought you had me
In that pit I jumped in
Thinking it would destroy me
Because of all my sins

I was so blind
Thinking "I have nothing to lose"
I willingly took the bait
The wrong path, I did choose

Thinking only of myself
As I wallowed in mud in mire
I really didn't care
Fulfilling, my fleshly desires

But when reality sat in
As I reaped, what I had sown
The sifting was so painful
If only I had known

The price I would pay
Would be so very high
Cost me almost everything
The Enemy really lied!

Like a burden too heavy
Weighed down in yuck
No one could pull me out
I felt like I was stuck

But then one blessed day
After many tears and pleas
I grab hold of the hand
That was reaching out to me

He said "I never left you
It's you who didn't trust
That everything you need
Is in all three of us

Father, Son, and Holy Spirit
We've been waiting on you
To finally see the light
And make the right move

You don't have to stay there
I'm here to tell you
The Enemy will make you believe
There is nothing you can do

But put your trust in Me
And don't have any doubt
Grasp hold of my hand
Yes, I will pull you out

Trust in the Lord with all your heart and lean not on your understanding; in all your ways acknowledge Him and He will make your paths straight.
Proverbs 3:5-6

It's Cop ascetic...

Yeah! It's all good
You lied, you mistreated me
You humiliated, and deceived me
You just plainly, didn't do right by me

But, it's all good
It's your lost
You see...
I am a **Good**
Kind
Loving
Caring Woman!
I am a woman of God
Who has much to offer
A well-deserved man
I know who I am, do you?

I am **Sage!**
Sassy!
Sensual!
Soulful!
Spiritual!
Sensational!
And most of all **Saved!**
As you see
I am the seven **S's**
Of God's craftsmanship

I want you to know
It was never about you
It's about Him!

So with all undue respect
Or that water thang...
"You don't miss your water
Until you well run dry"

I guess you better go find
Another waterfall
Because truly it is
Cop ascetic!

"My Girls"

We have the choice
To do what we feel
But members of my family
Weren't given an appeal

My two girls
Created the same day
Would make their exit
In the same way

A decision I'd make
That would grant me some peace
Because all of that worrying
Had to seize

Now perky and petite
Costly and round
My girls sit up
Tall like mounds

It's amazing how they look
My new set
They're not so bad
No reason for regret

I'm still all woman
With a little upgrade
Me and my girls
What a price we'd pay

Yes, it was worth it
Even the surgery
Thank God Almighty!
I'm now cancer free

The Lord will fulfill His purpose for; Your love,
O Lord, endures forever-do not abandon the works of Your
hands
Psalm 138:8

"RESURRECTION"

Taking my last breath
Nothing mattered
I would never deny Him
Even if my life was shattered

"I'll serve Him till I die"
Were the words that I spoke
As they surround me
To give the final blow

Within a second
A twinkling of an eye
This majestic light
Lift me through the sky

As I looked around
This unfamiliar place
Somehow I knew
That I was finally safe

Men from every nation
And every tongue
Would all greet me
I felt like I belong

I did ask the question
"Why so much pain?"
One said "He was stretching you
Some things couldn't remain "

He said "we know it was hard
At times you almost gave up
But because you persevered
You can now receive the cup

The promise will be fulfilled
Here's the gift of salvation
You past the test daughter
It's time for celebration!"

For you died, and your life is hidden with Christ." Col 3:23

"UNCONDITIONAL"

NO STRINGS ATTACHED
NO COMPROMISE
NO GIVE OR TAKES
OR FLAWS I'LL HIDE

IT IS, WHAT IT IS
ACCEPT IT OR NOT
I WON'T NEGOTIATE
I'VE GIVEN A LOT

THIS IS ME
GOD CRAFTED THIS WAY,
CAN'T YOU SEE MY HEART
WILL I EVER BE OKAY?

I WON'T SUCCUMB
ALTERATIONS, NO MORE
YOU CAN'T CHANGE ME
I HAVE MORE IN STORE

MY BEAUTY WITHIN
EXTENDS OUTSIDE
ENOUGH NIP AND TUCK
I DO HAVE SOME PRIDE

YES, IT'S MY CHOICE
A GIRLS PEROGATIVE
BUT HOW MUCH MORE
DO I HAVE TO GIVE?

UNCONDITIONAL
YOU SAID BACK THEN
OR WAS IT ALL LIES?
DID YOU JUST PRETEND?

ACCEPT ME FOR ME……

"Let you light shine before men, that they may see your good deeds and praise your Father In heaven."
Matthews 5:16

It Could be Worse

Facing foreclosure
Car repossessed
Handed a pink slip
Life's a total mess

Heartbroken
Family issues too
What's happening!
All Hell has broken loose!

Walking in circles
Can't sleep at night
Trying to understand
Why I'm in such a fight

Nearly insane
Living on the edge
I am in need of a lifeline
Or I'll soon be dead

A second wind
I so desperately need
I'm all choked up
I can barely breathe

Fighting in the spirit
And flesh too
This is not an easy task
For anyone to do

However;
There is a perfect Man
That holds me
In the hallow of His hand

Despite how it feels
I trust Him first
I will hold out
Things could be worse

*"Forgetting what lies behind... I press on
towards the goal." Philippians 3:13-14*

Delayed, Not Denied

Don't give up
It's on the way
Forget about what others
Have to say

It's coming!
He's working it out
Removing all the rubbish
That's stirring about

Listen,
One thing He can't do
And that is to lie
About what He has for you

Delayed;
Doesn't mean denied
Just trust Him
Stop questioning, why?

It's yours
No one can take it away
Forget about everything
And continue to pray

Claim it!
There is no need to fear
What He has for you
Nothing could interfere

It's yours...

*For the vision is yet for an appointed time; but at the end it
shall speak, and not lie; though it tarry, wait for it; because
it will surely come, it will not tarry.*
Habakkuk 2:3

"Its Over"

You said that you love me
You said that you cared
You said you were willing
To give your heart and share

"Inseparable we are"
You'd say time and time again
That we didn't need the world
That we were best friends

How could you be so treacherous?
Betray me the way you did
You really tried to hurt me
Destroy me in the end

After so many years
Enrage we would depart
Although good out-weighed the bad
It didn't touch your heart

You know I'd never hurt you
Despite what you've done
Remembering yesterday's love
To payback, I won't succumb

Yes, I forgive you
For everything you did
I pray you are delivered
But our story has to end

Father forgive them for they don't know
what they are doing."
Luke 23:24

"Thank You"

May I shake your hand?
Will you accept my embrace?
Can I nod with assurance?
One day face to face...

The storm has subsided
As I sail toward the next shore
No harshness of the wind
Un-balance waves no more

Forgetting yesterday
I'm headed toward tomorrow
Relishing each breeze
No more time for sorrow

I thank you, for the pressing
And the unpleasant release
Now I can truly sail
Toward destiny

Thank you...

Love keeps no record of wrongs.
1 Corinthians 13:5

Express your deepest thoughts:

1. Which poem was your favorite?
   Why?

2. Which poem can you relate to?
   How?

3. What poem inspired you the most?

Notes:

[Part Six]

Redemption!

*Therefore the redeemed of the Lord shall return,
and come with singing unto Zion;
And everlasting joy shall be upon their head;
They shall obtain gladness and joys;
And sorrow and mourning shall flee away.*

Isaiah 51:11

I Found Me!

Covered up
Hidden from myself
I discovered
This woman of wealth

Like a caterpillar
Finally out its cocoon
Metamorphosis took place
Not a minute too soon

I was always there
Just tucked away
For that perfect moment
On the perfect day

Now that I have arrived
Woman, lady, girl
I'm covered in the blood
On assignment for the world

Anointed and blessed
From head to toe
Wherever He leads
I will follow

I finally found me!
Yes, it took awhile
For me to realize
I was His chosen child

*"Whoever follows me will never walk in darkness,
but will have the light of life."
John 8:12*

FAVOR!

Oops! I'm smiling
What's come over me?
It's been so long
Am I finally free?

This is so juvenile
But listen, I've got to share
I feel so giddy and warm
I'm floating on Air

My inner being speaks
To not settle for less
What God's done for me
Truly is the best

It's His favor
That's fallen on me
I'm singing and dancing
Can this really be?

That the famine's is over
Restoration now in play
God has released His promises
He said He would one day

FAVOR, FAVOR, FAVOR!
God has given me
Things are better now
His grace has set me free

*Thou shalt arise and have mercy on upon Zion: for the time
to favor her,
Yea, the set time, is come
Psalm 102:13*

I Feel Good!

I feel good today
This is rare
Been so burden down
I'm finally coming up for air

I am actually content
No airs do I put on
In fact I feel good
Yesterday cares are gone

But I do wonder
Where this will lead
It's not often
That I get a chance to breathe

I'll absorb every moment
Tomorrow, I don't know
Things may be different
I have the past to show

I'm really feeling fine!
Can't worry about later
Nothing's been promised
To me life's never catered

For now I'll enjoy
What's been cast my way
Relishing every moment
And continuing to pray

Praise the Lord. Give thanks to the Lord, for He is good;
His love endures forever
Psalm 106:1

"New Skin"

This skin that I'm in
Has started to shed
Peeling away excess
Things that are dead

A new covering
Is replacing the old
It's a new me
Looking good I'm told

A spanking new radiance
I now possess
An unexplainable glow
Has replaced the stress

That old skin I was in
Was vulnerable and weak
Blemished by life
It was too meek

But that day came
When I said, "enough is enough"!
I decided to change
My skin became tough

Oh! I look splendid
Inside and out
Only God really knows
What this is about

Look at me now
Do you like what you see?
I'm out of my cocoon
I'm a brand new me

Therefore, if anyone is in Christ, he is a new creation;
the old has gone, the new has come.
2 Corinthians 5:17

"UNEXPLAINABLE"

What is this feeling?
Deep inside of me
That makes me shout
"I got the victory!"

An awesome sensation
If I only could explain
What's going on within
Replacing all the pain

I don't understand
Where it came from
All I know is
It makes me want to run!

Tried over and over
To figure it out
This unexplainable desire
That leaves no room for doubt

Yes, I've been touched
Healed and changed
Filled with a power
He only could arrange

Oh, how I thank Him
For stirring up my soul
I can now say, I am finally whole

Praise the Lord. Praise God in His sanctuary...
Praise Him for His acts of power...
Praise Him with the sounding of the trumpet...
Let everything that has breath praise the Lord.
Psalm 1:50

Woman of God

Bold, brave
Beautiful, bless
Called according to purpose
Set apart from the rest

Woman of God
Standing on the front line
Warrior of the word
Representing the divine

Spiritual and strong
Yet sweet to the soul
Wise enough to know
Who's totally in control

Girded up in armor
Ready, come what may
Exemplifying Phenomenal
In each and every way

An heir to the throne
A queen she's perceived
No matter where she goes
She displays royalty

Woman of God
Loyal to the end
Fulfilling destiny
Standing against the wind

"Daughter, your faith has healed you.
Go in peace and be freed from your suffering."
Mark 5:3

SHEROE'

What kind of woman
In the world is this?
Hell has no fury
Life has no bliss

Born to Fight!
Strong and wise
The gift of long-suffering
Has been her prize

Discolored...
"Pain" is her name
Exclusively Chosen
To bear life's stains

Sheroe'
Pride tries to break her down
Conspiring and Plotting
To make her relinquish her crown

With a Golden heart
Silver even yields
Often wondering
What is the deal?

Fight on Woman!
Sent solely from above
You are symbolic
Of God's amazing love

God is my strength and power;
and he maketh my way perfect.
2 Samuel 22:33

A Friend Indeed...

Through the years I'd pray
For someone like you
A real true friend
That last, through and through

Many would come
But time always reveal
Their true hearts
And how they really feel

Counterfeits and phonies
Pretenders they would be
Took my kindness for weakness
They tried to use me

But here comes Lady Sunshine
A name that describes
The warmth and kindness
That's lighten up so many lives

You are an instrument
A vessel of God's love
With treasures and blessings
Stored up above

I do thank-you
For all you've done for me
Having a real friend
Feels good, yes indeed...

Two are better than one, because they have a good return
forTheir work; if one falls down, his friend can help him up.
Ecclesiastes 4:9-10

Mister...

Unexpectedly he came
At the perfect time
I never thought I'd meet
Someone so fine

Simply, exclusive
Filled with love
Wise as a serpent
Humble as a dove

Oooh! I am so excited
Wonder what's his next move?
There's something about him
He got this special groove

I really don't know
Won't even try and guess
All I know is
I am truly impressed

For now I will enjoy
What's been cast my way
All bets are off
I am ready to play

Mister...
You may not understand
That you might be
My extraordinary man

"What kind of man is this?"
Matthew 8:27

Simply, Redeemed

I was bought with a purpose
Purchase by a King
Paid for with His blood
My soul has been redeemed

He lifted me
Out of despair
Filled me with His love
Overcame me with care

Simply redeemed
Delivered and changed
It feels real good
To be given a new name

Unspeakable joy
My soul has been set free
I am now walking
Into my destiny

Glory Hallelujah!
I give all praises to You
Redeemed, redeemed
I'm simply, redeemed

My lips will shout for joy when I sing praises to you,
I whom you have redeemed.
Psalm 71:23

Victory!

This blessing
Is truly divine
Showed up!
At the perfect time

Unbelievable
I'm on top of the world
My Father looked out
For His precious girl

I can't stop smiling
It feels so good
To finally win
And be understood

I want to dance!
I want to sing!
Just open my window
I want to scream!

Can't keep it to myself!
I have to tell
That when you trust Him
You shall prevail!

Thank you Lord!
You are the best
Forever in your arms
I will surely rest

Looking at them, Jesus said "With men it is impossible, but not with God, because all things are possible with God."
Mark 10:27

Thankful!

Oh Happy day!
I thought you would never come
With arms open wide
I can now feel the sun

There is food on the table
Gas in the tank
My bills are paid
With a few dollars in the bank

My family is doing better
Boss is not as bad
Children are well
I'm really feeling glad

It feels like spring time
Although its fall
I have waited for this moment
To finally stand tall

Yes, I'm so thankful
Life feels right
You said if I would hold out
That day, would replace the night

Sing joyfully to the Lord, you righteous;
It is fitting for the upright to praise Him.
Psalm 33:1

"The Finish Line"

Yes, I made it!
Just in time
I finally cross
The finish line

The roads were narrow
The hills very steep
Passing through the valleys
Sometimes I would weep

Still pressing on
At times taking a rest
Not knowing which direction
Would be best

But love showed up
Grace, my companion
Faith stayed around
I was never abandon

Peace flowed aside
Mercy held me up
Perseverance challenge me
To get the winning cup

Now that I've crossed
I am now set free
From all those burdens
That had its hold on me

Yes! I made it
Just in the nick of time
It really feels good
To cross the finish line

I have fought the good fight, I have finished the race,
and I have kept the faith
2 Timothy 4:7

Express your deepest thoughts:

1. Which poem was your favorite?
   Why?

2. Which poem can you relate to?
   How?

3. What poem inspired you the most?

Notes:

Short

Testimonials...

For we are not as many, which corrupt the word of God: but as of sincerity, but as of God, in the sight of God speak we in Christ.
2 Corinthians 2:17

The Vision

That glow…as I look at the doorpost and gaze at the flickering

sparkles; I wonder, what the hell is going on! I rub the sleep

from my eyes, shake my head, and can't believe what's right

in front of me. In clear view, I'm witnessing the eighth wonder

of the world, here inside my bedroom. Amazed at the sight, I

yell out to my visiting cousin, "look, don't you see what I see,

those burning candles, where did they come from?" She

responds back, "girl you crazy, you're just dreaming, ain't no

candles burning, go back to sleep." I try to convince her of

what I'm seeing. Calling me crazy again, she mumbles, turns

over and goes back to sleep. Being immature and oblivious

to many things in life, I had no idea I was experiencing my

first spiritual encounter. God was sending me a message

through those candles; He clearly wanted my attention and

me. As I lie there mesmerized, yet unafraid, I knew there had

to be an answer to this. God placed that vision in my

bedroom for a reason. Perhaps one day I will understand as

it manifest itself in my life.

Why Me Lord?

I had planned on sitting in my warm bath and cry my eyes out to get rid of the pain, but I never made it that far. You know they say, "You'll feel better once you let it all out, crying cleanses the soul". In my nakedness, I fall across the bed and allow the floodgates to open. As the tears and saliva meet each other in the center of my pillow, I shout, "why me Lord? Why are you allowing me to suffer so? Why won't you make everything all right? Why haven't you answered my pleas?" Immediately, the Holy Spirit speaks back, "why not you". I respond, "I'll do anything you want me to do, go anywhere you want me to go, if you just stop this merry-go-round of pain. Simply, just make it all go away?" I then hear another voice, and it speaks one word, "persevere." As I lift up my head and turn toward the television to see who so eloquently spoke that word, I knew that the Lord was at work, because that man of God read my soul! He stated, "God loves you, and haven't forgotten about you. You must believe, He's allowing this for a reason. Although you're in the fire, like pure gold you're going to come out smooth, polished, and new. Yes, it doesn't feel good and there is much you don't understand, but you must **Stand** and know that victory shall be yours. Everything you've lost child will be returned tenfold." He also stated, "He wouldn't bring you this far to leave you." "Oh yes, I agree"! I said. Suddenly, I felt hope! I felt strengthen! I felt empowered! I felt GOD! I will trust Him! I am more than a conqueror! To God be the GLORY!!!

Breathe Again

Whew! "I can do this. The bible says, "I can do all things through Christ who strengthens me." As I struggle to take my next breath, I look back and wonder; "*how did I make it this far?*" All the struggles I have had to face over the years. I know it was only the blood of Jesus that carried me, and still is. But in the natural, I can't understand how I am making it. Spiritually, I must use any means necessary to beat this thing. The odds are not in my favor. They say, "no way, no how." But, suddenly something comes over me, and I shout aloud, "they don't know the God that I serve; **He** is my Alpha and Omega! **He** is my bright and Morning Star! And yes, even that **Doctor** in a sick room! **He** is **GOD!** I will take my chances on **Him**. **He** will heal me, free me, and deliver me. Then finally I will breathe again.

HELP!

"What's happening? Why have you forsaken me? Please answer me Father!" Oh, how I cried out those words in the midst of my brokenness. I'm a good girl; I don't hurt anyone. I love my family and I serve you God, why are you allowing me to go through all of this? You can do something to change this situation, You're God. You can blow one breath and make everything right. Why won't you rescue me? You say you love me, you say you'll never leave or forsake me. Don't you hear me Father? I'm calling your name! Again, He reminds me that things are done on His time, not mine. He knows all and sees all. He cannot lie and will do just what He says. He's *pruning me, purging me, and preparing me to get the best out of me.* I must *persevere*. I also, must allow Him to break off some old behaviors, habits, and uncanny natures so He can use me to the fullest. It's not about me world it's about HIM! I must trust and wait on HIM. Yes, Help is on the way.

OBEDIENCE

Why am I so hardheaded? Sometimes, I'm just a bit stubborn. I try to do what's right, but the flesh shows up, and I succumb to the wrong. Why does life have so many rules anyway? How about those commandments, aren't they hard to follow at times? Well, it's my life; wouldn't I know what's best for me? Oh well, you don't understand, nor do I, but He does. He knows everything, and is everything. He knows how many hairs are on my head. He knows my inner and outer being. He even knew me, before I was conceived in my Mother's womb. So, why won't I just completely obey Him? Surrender my all to Him? Just be a good daughter, and follow Him? But again, I'm a little hardheaded. I should've learned by now? Once more I find myself back in those uncomfortable situations again. Yes, it's true; obedience is better than sacrifice. I for one should know.

"It Takes All Three"

Here we go again...."leave me alone, and stop touching me!"
This warfare is starting to get on my last nerve. As I reach for
my bible and place it under my pillow, I try to gather my thoughts
to remember where I put the anointing oil, because I'm going to
need it tonight. Out loud, I begin to plead the blood of Jesus,
and rebuke every unclean spirit, including sending them back to
hell as I sling the oil and pray for a peaceful night sleep. It's sad,
but my prerequisite for going to sleep at night, consist of this type
of ritual. As I continue to shout, I can actually feel and see the
place in my mattress being lifted as it flee my presence. You see
darkness and light, or good and evil can't mix, so as I go along
speaking the word and of course slinging oil, it has to take flight.
How I got to this point of boldness and courage, I really couldn't
tell you. All I know is, I was fed up with sleepless nights in my
home, and I knew I had to do something, to bring normalcy back
to my life again. Allowing God to direct my path, I had to take a
stance, and believe I would come out these undeserved attacks
with victory. Believe me; I'm not so cocky or crazy enough to
think that I can beat this thing alone, Oh no, the Devil has
thousands of years of experience, and is the master of

deceit. Listen, this stuff is real. Satan is real. He sends his spirits, witches, warlocks, imps, demons, and people to try and steal your joy, destroy your life, kill your purpose and maybe even you! These things exist, and if someone tells you they don't, you better pray the blinders are taken off of them and they're delivered. I'm a living testimony that it does exist. Yes, I was afraid to talk about it at first and thought everyone would call me crazy, but I had to trust God, step out on faith and expose it for what it is. Remember God has given you some weaponry. First, the **blood** of Jesus is real, and will never lose its power. Secondly, the **anointing oil** heals, delivers, and protects, but it has supremacy. But most of all, His **word** is sharper than a two-edged sword. Utilize all three of these, and you will have victory. Trust me; God will do exactly what He says people. He will cover you, keep you, and set you free. Allow him to come in and fight these adversaries for you. All this evil is trying to do is place that emotion of fear in you, to hinder your purpose, or even stop you from getting to your destiny. You are a chosen vessel! You are God's instrument of love! But most of all, you are a child of the King! What God has for you, is for you! There is no Devil in hell that can keep you from it, if you trust God to do exactly what He says.

I Won't Quit!

I don't know what's going on. But lately, I haven't been feeling my best. I wonder were all this is going to end up. I feel weary, tired and just plain fed up. The flesh is weak, and I don't know how much longer I can hold out. I know that the enemy has his hand in this. I've asked God to sustain me, and order my steps. I'm praying for a miracle. I have to wait on God, but I must admit, I'm at my wits end. When I got in tonight from church, the house was very quiet. I quickly took my warm bath and afterwards tried to settle in for the night. As I thought back on the events of my evening, and how I felt sitting in church, it only made me discouraged. It's like, this thing is not only affecting my home, but also my worship. God please help me! As I pop the two Tylenol p.m.'s into my mouth I think, *this is really sad*, I can't even fall asleep on my own, without some over the counter sleep aid. I've given so much to one person. I've fought so hard for my marriage. I've lost so much of myself, and for what!   He says he don't want to be delivered. He say's stop trying to save something that doesn't want to be saved. He says he has freewill. So why can't I just give up on him?   One thing I know for sure is that I can't accept the old man back. Eventually, that man will spiritually, emotionally, and maybe physically kill me.

Lord, I need a renewed husband, a new life, a new me! I will not accept anything less than that. As I feel his hand rub my bottom, I think to myself, "have he lost his mind". This man mistreats me, and now he wants to make love, Oh hell no, not this time! I begin to pray. Father, if you did not ordain this, please don't allow it to happen. It's 1:00 a.m. in the morning, what the hell is he trying to prove. Well, anyway it happened; but God is good, it was one of those quickies (about five minutes). I awake to my husband kissing me on the cheek. Saying good-bye, I quickly return to sleep and go into a deep dream. In the dream, I'm in a big field and there is a big tree filled with lots of fruit and a stream of blue water nearby. The large size fruit looks like a combination of an orange and a mango. I wanted to pick one, but I said, "this fruit is overly ripe". Suddenly, a group of men appeared and ask, "May we have some of your fruit"? I respond "of course"! The men of different nationalities seem to enjoy my fruit. They talked of its beautiful color, size, and sweetness. Across the river I notice two other trees, but they're brown, bear with no leaves. I believe those trees represented two people, one I know of, the other, I'm not sure. What an awesome dream with such vivid colors. I know God is setting things up and doing something in my life. As usual, I'll continue to wait and trust Him.

Sleeping with the Enemy

As I lay next to him and look out the corner of my eye, that song keeps playing in my head, "There's a stranger in my house... It took a while to figure out... That he wasn't who he said he was...He's got to be someone else... Because, he wouldn't touch me like that...And treat me like he does." Although, I carry his last name, I'm having a problem figuring out, exactly who he is. The word says "the enemy comes to kill, steal, and destroy," could he be the enemy? When I think back to the day he stole my heart, I truly felt like cupid had aimed its arrow right at me. I trusted this stranger, I believed this stranger, and I even fell in love with this stranger. I wonder what this stranger wants from me. Is there anything left for him to take? He stole my heart, shattered my dreams, and destroyed our love. I've got to find a way, to get away, from this stranger who obviously is... the **Enemy!**

I MARRIED SATAN'S SON

Oh no! Not another one. My nerves are so bad that my skin is breaking out, and my hair is falling out too. And to top it all off, this morning while showering, I found two, not one lump in my right breast. My God what's next? I'll suffer for your kingdom, I'll do whatever you want, but this warfare is a bit too much. Well, I sort of bought it on myself. You see, I stepped outside of God's will. I, without consulting Him, decided that I was going to marry and live happily ever after with a man that I loved more than water. I chose an unequally yoked partner. I loved someone who didn't love himself. I gave every part of me to someone who couldn't give back. I married Satan's Son! Living in this hell has caused me to lose so much. I lost my joy! I lost my peace! I lost some friends! But most of all, I've almost lost my mind! Jumping into this pit has nearly ruined my life. Although money isn't an issue, I would give up this two-story house, this brand new Mercedes Benz, these three closets of clothing, and this platinum diamond ring, to have my old life back. I allowed blind love and disobedience to bankrupt me. I made a mistake. I married Satan's Son.

WHAT'S NEXT?

I can't move. I won't move. I'm safe underneath this blanket. I don't want to face anyone. I don't want to talk to anybody. I don't want to pretend everything is all right, anymore. I'm safe here. But slowly, reality creeps in and reminds me; life is waiting and its time to come out of hiding. If my Mama only knew my pain, if my Daddy could make it right like when I scrapped my knee as a child. If God would just pick me up and rock mc in His bosom. If I could just get over this thang! Oh God, "What's next", I wonder? Your word says, "Weeping endures for a night, but joy comes in the morning." I can't wait until that sunbeam of life shine on me? When will grace and mercy shower down? When will that unspeakable joy find its way to my soul? Still covered in the full armor of God, I will wait for the "Next", trusting and believing, He will deliver, just like He said.

If They Only Knew

As I walk through the corridors of my workplace, make-up flawless, haired combed with each string in place, outfit in unison with shoes and purse, to the world she's got it altogether…. in other words "the sister got it going on!" Proceeding to the bathroom to make sure my lipstick hasn't rested on my whitened teeth; I stare at the facade of a woman in the mirror and say to myself, "If they only knew." Again, I wonder *how someone as intelligent, attractive, and caring could become a victim of abuse.* Thinking back on last night's ordeal, I try to figure out, *what's wrong with me? Why won't I leave? Why can't I let go? When will I put a halt to this merry-go-round of pain? Simply God; why can't I stop loving him?* I say to myself, *"Girl you deserve better."* But, those demons show up again reminding me of my weaknesses. Help me God, rescue me Father, save me Jesus! Lastly, I swallow, exhale and remind myself, *they don't know.* But perhaps, they do.

~All Is *Forgiven*~

It is truly amazing, how time heals all things. From an open wound, to a shattered heart, time is the best remedy. With time, I have to move on to the next. I will forget what's over my shoulder. I will relinquish any attached emotions. *I forgive you*. **Deep down** inside, I believe you tried. I also believe, **deep down,** you really cared. But most of all, **deep down,** I know you loved me, in your own special way. *I forgive you*. You know, God gave His only son to die for our sins and despite how we've treated Him **He forgives us**. I pray one day, the blinders come off, and you see who the enemy really is. I also pray that complete deliverance and salvation come your way. But most of all, I pray that you believe, I **always** had your best interest. You probably won't believe what I'm saying, but it doesn't matter anymore. **All is forgiven**. Lastly, I pray one day, **you'll forgive** me too. Be blessed, and I truly wish you Peace and Love.

"My Open Vision"

~THE THRONE ROOM~

MY GOD! Where am I? Looking around, I'm in awe at what surrounds me. It's the most beautiful sight one could ever imagine. As I pinch myself to try and figure out, is this real; I hear a powerful, yet calm voice that spoke," Valerie, It's your Father, I don't want you to think you're dreaming". I turn toward the direction of the voice, but there is no one there. He then states, "Everything is going to be alright, I'm here now". I can't explain that feeling, all I know is; I never felt so much peace, so safe, and so loved. Again He speaks, "you mean to tell me she's still going through, give her everything she needs! Give her rubies and diamonds, pearls and emeralds, sapphires and gold. **Give her everything!"** Still in amazement, I look around at my surroundings. The gold/orange colored walls seem to jump out at me. The tall gold vases shined ever so brightly. The treasure chests sitting on the floor was filled with jewels and gold coins overflowing. The beautiful gold colored artifacts were an unexplainable sight. I couldn't believe what I was actually seeing. My God, what could I have done to deserve such a journey like this? Why would He reveal all of this to a sinner like me? I then turn and spoke words I can't remember to that voice. But, I do remember this. I have never felt so much love, happiness; no other time in my life did everything so perfect. Suddenly, after my spiritual journey, I was back lying in my bed. As I cried through the rest of the night, I thought, you know; I'll trade my entire lifetime, for another visit like that with my Father. I'm still in awe...

I Stand!

Refusing to let go of God's unchanging hand
My steps are ordered by Him...

I Stand!

Defeating the odds, those that are against me, healed by an
awesome God
By His stripes I am healed...

I Stand!

Through the storms of life, sheltered by grace and mercy
Through Him my strength is made perfect in my
weaknesses...

I Stand!

With my head held high, forgetting those things which are
behind
I am running the race and reaching toward those things
destined for me...

I Stand!

On His word, petitioning and reminding Him of the promises
His word does not come back void and He cannot lie...

I Stand!

Putting my trust totally in Him, I will not fear what flesh can do
unto me
He has not given me the spirit of fear...

I Stand!

Healed, Anointed, Appointed, Audacious, Blessed, Strong,
and Saved...

I STAND!

"A Special Invitation"

If you have read this book and you have not received Jesus as your Savior, I beseech you to make a decision right now. It does not matter where you are, and what is going on in your life, Jesus is waiting to receive you, as you receive Him. He truly loves you and is waiting for you to make Him Lord of your life. Just take the first step, by saying, "yes" to Him, and He will take care of the rest. Now with your heart and mind fixed on Him, say this simple prayer

"LORD JESUS I BELIEVE THAT YOU DIED FOR ME AT CALVARY.
I RECEIVE YOU NOW AS MY SAVIOR AND LORD,
COME LIVE IN MY HEART!"

If you have said this prayer, you are now
Saved!
Rejoice, for the Angels in heaven are rejoicing over your **Salvation!**
Lastly, join yourself to a local body of believers who are preaching and teaching that Jesus is Lord, and He is the Christ.

God Bless You!

"Contact Information"

STAND WOMAN STAND!

<u>Specialty:</u>
Life Coach
Spiritual Wellness
Women Empowerment
Inspirational/Motivational Speaking
Cancer Support Mentor

If you would like to share how this book has help or encouraged you, or if you would like to consult with Valerie individually for a group or organization speaking engagement/ conference/ workshop/ book signing, etc. please contact:
<u>vgoldenallen@gmail.com</u> or
<u>vjpublishinghouse@gmail.com</u>

Email all other correspondence to:

Literary Agent: Stephanie Sills
sillsstudy@aol.com

Assistant: Durrell Knight
durrellknight@bellsouth.net

www.ingramcontent.com/pod-product-compliance
Lightning Source LLC
LaVergne TN
LVHW041225080426
835508LV00011B/1083